Library of Congress Cataloging-in-Publication Data

Watts, Barrie.
    Mushroom.

    (Stopwatch books)
    Includes index.
    Summary: Discusses the parts of mushrooms and how these fungi grow.
        1. Mushrooms—Juvenile literature. [1. Mushrooms]
I. Title. II. Series.
QK617.W37 1986   589.2'223   86-6659
ISBN 0-382-09301-1
ISBN 0-382-09287-2 (lib. bdg.)

First published by A & C Black (Publishers) Limited
35 Bedford Row, London WC1R 4JH

© 1986 Barrie Watts

First published in the United States in 1986
by Silver Burdett Company
Morristown, New Jersey

Acknowledgements
The artwork is by Helen Senior.
The publishers would like to thank Jean Imrie for her help and advice.

Mushroom

Barrie Watts

Stopwatch books

 Silver Burdett Company • Morristown, New Jersey

These mushrooms are good to eat.

Have you ever eaten mushrooms like these? Look at their different shapes. Some are button mushrooms and some are flat mushrooms.

Here are a button mushroom and a flat mushroom.

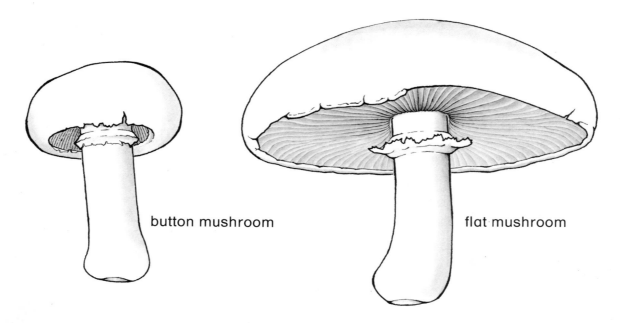

button mushroom

flat mushroom

The button mushroom was picked when it was young.
The flat mushroom was picked when it was older.
It has grown bigger than the button mushroom.

This book shows you how a mushroom grows.

This is where mushrooms grow.

These wild mushrooms are growing in a field.

Wild mushrooms come up once a year. You can find them in early autumn when the weather is warm and damp. Never eat them unless a grownup says they are all right.

Look at the big photograph. These mushrooms are growing on a special mushroom farm. They can grow here all year round. The mushrooms we eat usually come from mushroom farms like this one.

The mushroom has a stalk and a cap.

Here is a mushroom growing in the soil. The bottom part of the mushroom is called the stalk. On top of the stalk is the cap. The cap is shaped a bit like an umbrella.

You can't see all of the mushroom in this photograph. Part of it grows under the ground, like this.

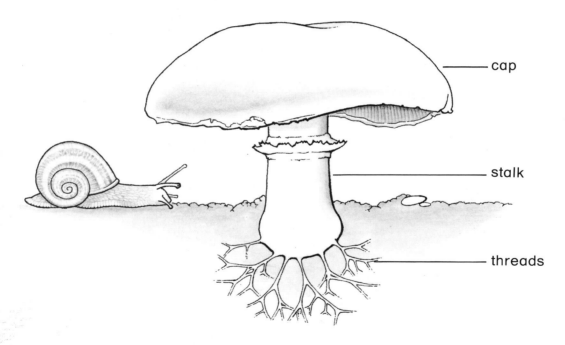

cap

stalk

threads

The stalk is joined to little threads in the ground.
The threads take in water and food from the soil.
The mushroom needs food and water to live.

Under the cap there are gills.

Underneath the mushroom cap there are lots of thin flaps.
They are called gills. Look at the big photograph.
The gills are dark brown. They are covered in tiny
brown specks, called spores.

You can't see the spores in the photograph. But if you
put a mushroom cap down on a piece of paper, some of
the spores will drop out, like this.

The pattern which they make is called a spore print.

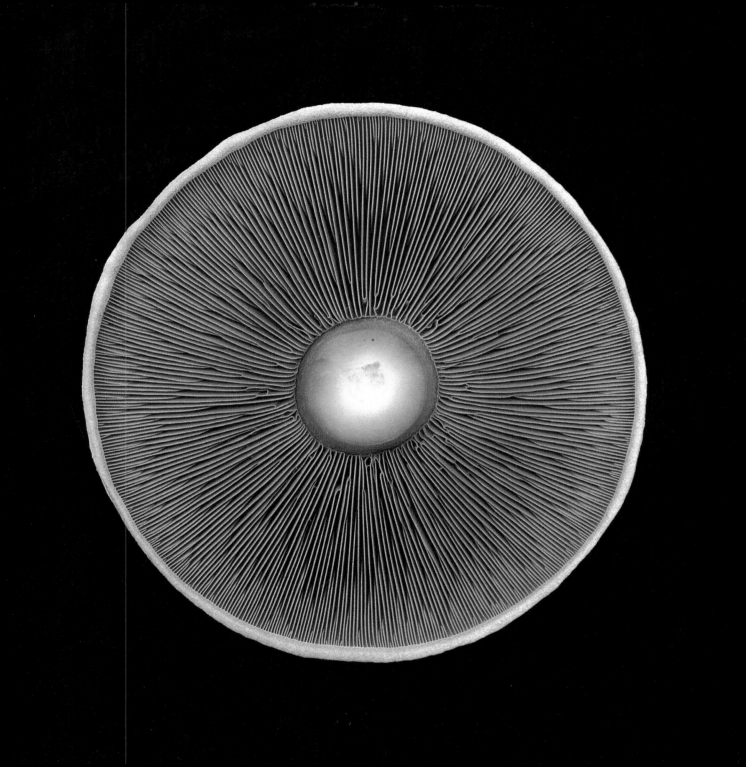

Spores grow on the gills.

This mushroom cap has been cut down the middle.
Can you see the brown gill? It is covered with spores.
Thousands of spores can grow on each gill.

This picture shows the spores very large.

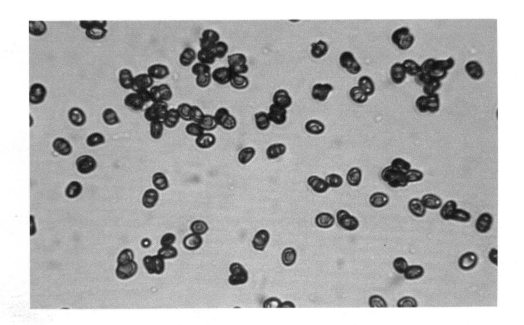

In real life, thousands and thousands of these tiny
spores would fit onto the head of a pin.

When the spores are fully grown, they fall off the gills.

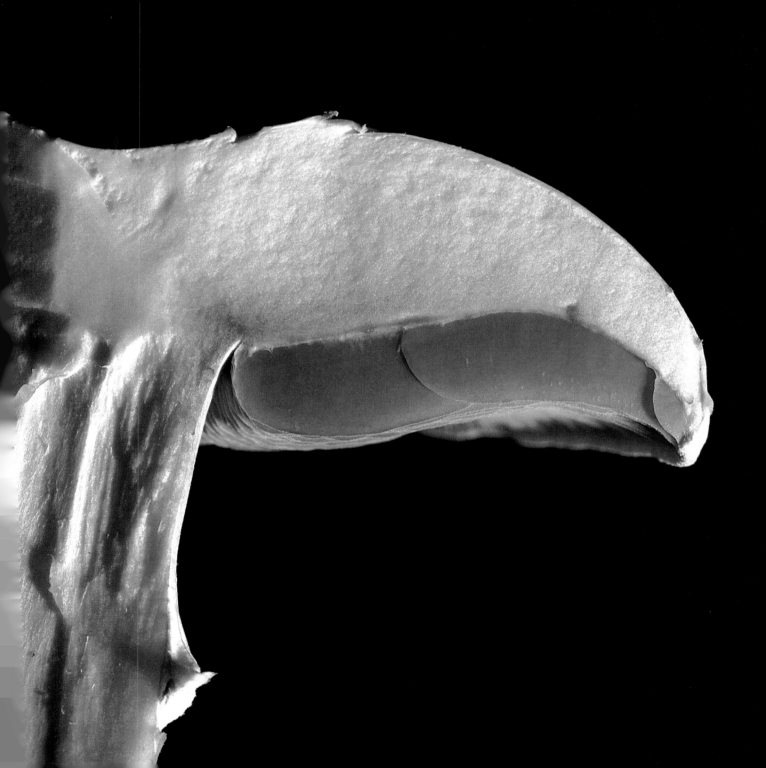

Threads grow from the spores.

The spores are very light so the wind carries them away from the mushroom.

Sometimes a spore lands on damp soil. Then tiny threads come out from the spore, like this.

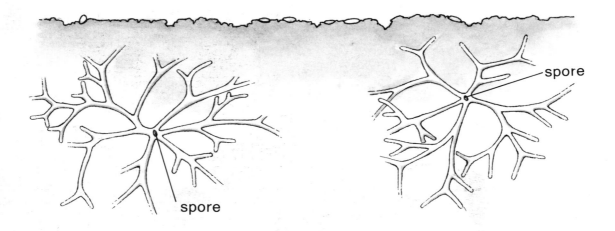

Look at the photograph. The threads are growing. They look a bit like cotton thread.

A new mushroom grows from the threads.

Sometimes two threads meet in the soil. Then a mushroom starts to grow. Look at the drawing.

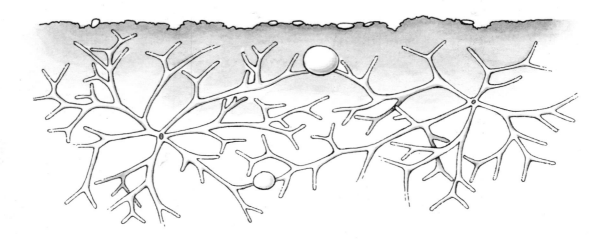

Where two threads join there is a bump. Soon the bump swells up into a button. This will be a new mushroom.

Look at the photograph. Can you see the new mushroom? There are other new mushrooms growing nearby. They are pushing up through the soil.

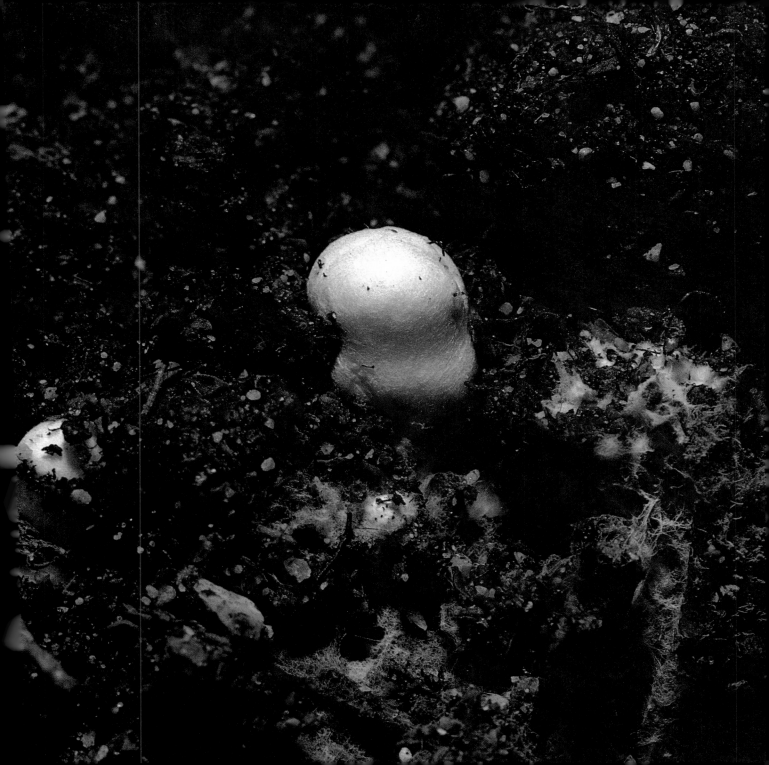

The mushroom grows above the ground.

If the weather is warm and damp the mushroom grows very quickly. In one day it can double in size.

Here is the mushroom cut down the middle.

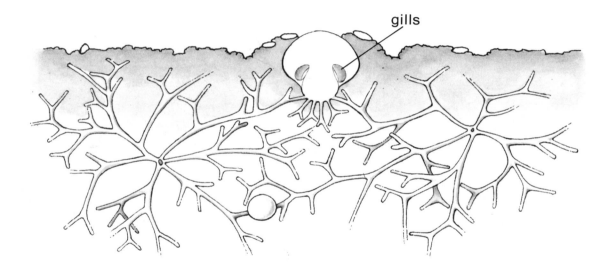

Can you see the gills growing inside it?

Look at the photograph. The mushroom has pushed up through the top of the soil.

The cap breaks away from the stalk.

Look at the drawing. Can you see where the outside of the cap is joined to the stalk?

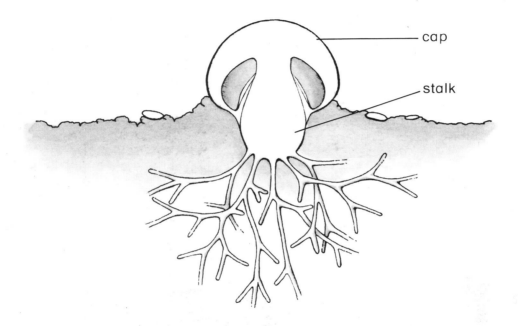

cap

stalk

As the button mushroom swells up, the cap breaks away from the stalk. Some of the cap is left on the stalk. This is called the ring.

Now look at the photograph. Can you see the ring on this mushroom?

The cap gets flatter.

Now the mushroom cap is almost flat. If you look under the cap you can see the gills.

At first the gills are pink. But they soon turn brown. Look at the big photograph. Spores are growing on the gills.

The mushroom is old.

Slugs and snails like to eat mushrooms. They make holes in the mushroom cap.

Soon the mushroom gets old and dry. Its spores blow away in the wind. Some of the spores will land on warm damp soil. What do you think will happen to them?

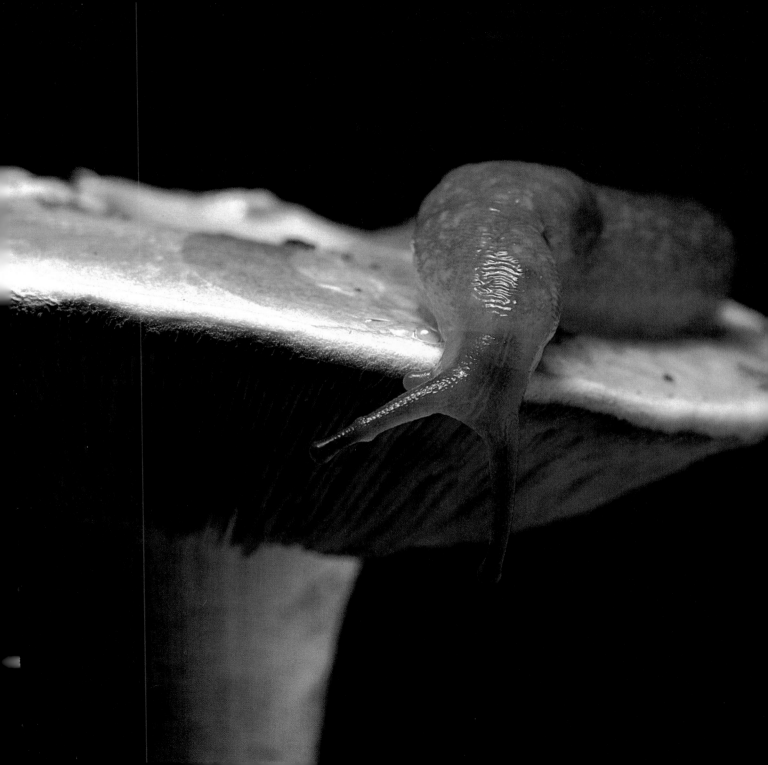

Do you remember how a mushroom grows?
See if you can tell the story in your own words.
You can use these pictures to help you.

3

6

Gently put a mushroom cap with the gills facing downward
on a piece of white paper. Leave it overnight. When you
lift the cap you will have a spore print.
Never pick and eat mushrooms unless you are with a grownup.

589.2   Watts, Barrie
Wa
         Mushroom

DATE DUE

Mar 15			
Mar 16			
Feb 5			
Oct 23			

THERE'S AN ANT IN ANTHONY

BY BERNARD MOST

William Morrow and Company   New York 1980

Copyright© 1980 by Bernard Most

Library of Congress Cataloging in Publication Data

Most, Bernard.   There's an ant in Anthony.

Summary: After discovering an "ant" in his own name,
Anthony searches for the word "ant" in other words.
[1. Vocabulary—Fiction] I. Title.
PZ7.M8544Th   [E]   79-23089
ISBN 0-688-22226-9   ISBN 0-688-32226-3 lib. bdg.

Printed in the United States of America.
1 2 3 4 5 6 7 8 9 10

To Amy with love,
for all your help.

Anthony was learning
how to spell his name in school one day
when he found an ant in Anthony.

Since he had found an ant in his name,
Anthony wondered
if he could find ants in other things.

So he searched all over his room.
He did not find an ant in a pair of pajamas,
or an ant in a goldfish bowl,
or an ant in a chest of drawers.

But he kept looking,
and he found an ant in a plant.

He searched in his backyard.
He did not find an ant in a barbecue,
or an ant in a lawn sprinkler,
or an ant in a hammock.

But he found an ant in a radio antenna.

He searched in the city.
He did not find an ant in a skyscraper,
or an ant in a crowd,
or an ant in a traffic jam.

He found an ant in a fire hydrant.

He searched the circus.
He did not find an ant in a flying trapeze,
or an ant in a clown,
or an ant in a bag of peanuts.

But he found an ant in an elephant.

He was getting hungry,
so he searched a fruit stand.
He did not find an ant in a banana,
or an ant in a piece of watermelon,
or an ant in a tangerine.

Surprise!
He found an ant in a cantaloupe.

He searched the zoo, too.
He did not find an ant in a panda bear,
or an ant in an armadillo,
or an ant in a kangaroo.

Instead, he found an ant in a panther.

He searched a haunted house.
He did not find an ant in a spiderweb,
or an ant in a skeleton,
or an ant in a bat.

Don't be scared.
He found an ant in a phantom.

He went to the library
and searched through some fairy tales.
He did not find an ant in a dragon,
or an ant in a knight in shining armor,
or an ant in a magic beanstalk.

He found an ant in a giant.

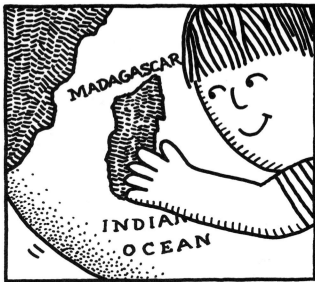
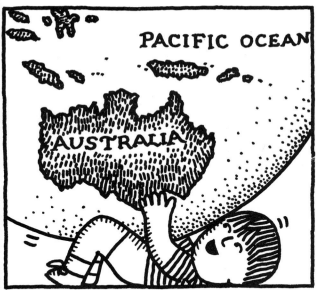

He searched around the globe.
He did not find an ant in Madagascar,
or an ant in Australia,
or an ant in Bermuda.

Of all places,
he found an ant in the Atlantic.

He searched the African jungle.
He did not find an ant in a crocodile,
or an ant in a hippopotamus,
or an ant in a ten-foot python.

But he did find an ant in an antelope.

He searched the North Pole.
He did not find an ant in a snowball,
or an ant in an explorer,
or an ant in a team of reindeer.

Of course, he found an ant in Santa.

He searched among all kinds of shapes.
He did not find an ant in a rectangle,
or an ant in a circle,
or an ant in a octagon.

But he looked some more,
and he found an ant in a slant.

Anthony was very tired
after finding so many ants,
so he sat down on the grass to rest.

Without looking for them,
he found ants in his pants.

He had found enough ants for one day,
he thought,
so he ran home that instant.

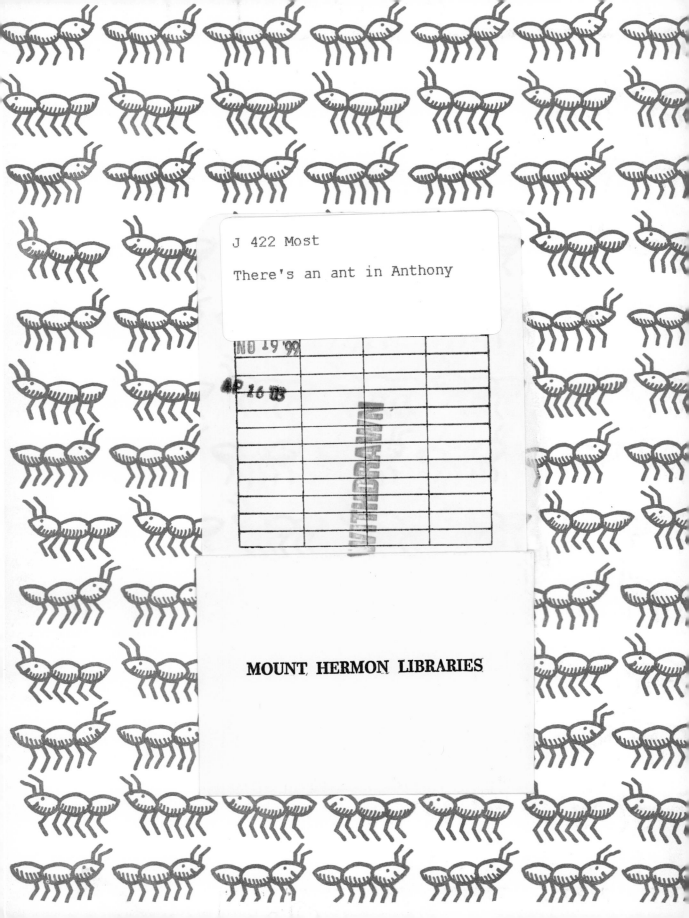